Calligraphy

A HANDBOOK FOR BEGINNERS

Calligraphy

A HANDBOOK FOR BEGINNERS

Beverley Amos

SIMON & SCHUSTER

AUSTRALIA

Acknowledgments

My grateful thanks to: Joy Blakeney for her assistance and patience with typing; William Lai, for generously providing pens and inks for our photographs, from his vast range at Will's Quills, Chatswood; Hazel Fletcher for contributing the artwork on page 78; one of my Springwood students for the contributions on pages 37, 48, 77 and 79; Kay and Tony Nixon for lending the piece on page 90 and Jenny Wager for the piece on page 91; Ruth Venner, Gemma Black, Bill Sippo, Christine Farmer, Roy Weston, Elaine Witton and Pat Gittins for recommending suppliers; Jill Osborne for reading and commenting on the manuscript; and to my patient and understanding editor, Ariana Klepac, for her forbearance.

CALLIGRAPHY

First published in Australasia in 1989 by
Simon & Schuster Australia
7 Grosvenor Place, Brookvale NSW 2100

A division of Gulf + Western

© Beverley Amos, 1989

National Library of Australia
Cataloguing in Publication data

Amos, Beverley.
  Calligraphy, a handbook for beginners.

  Bibliography.
  Includes index.
  ISBN 0 7318 0054 0.

  1. Calligraphy – Amateurs' manuals. I. Title.

745.6'1'0240909

Designed by Michelle Havenstein
Typeset in Bembo by Savage Type Pty Ltd
Printed in Singapore by Toppan Printing Pte Limited

Foreword

 HIS slim volume has been eagerly awaited by many calligraphers.

The book has been designed for the use of new calligraphers, especially those unable to take classes. The text is simple, clear and succinct.

Calligraphy — A Handbook for Beginners takes the new student carefully through the rudiments of the craft — the lessons that must be learnt before one can become an informed and confident writer. It is thus a short step to take full advantage of Part Four — putting your new skill into practice.

The author's teaching experience has enabled her to identify the common pitfalls we all have to negotiate as beginners. Her gentle style makes the progress smooth and encouraging.

Bev Amos' own exposure to international calligraphy gives her a confidence in her subject which is evident in her writing style. This is a valuable book for those looking for strong guidance as a new calligrapher, whether for personal use or commercial application.

Jill Osborne
President
Australian Society of Calligraphers

DEDICATION

To my wonderful family
for their unfailing love and confidence,
also my friends and students
in both Springwood and Katoomba
who gave me
such moral support and encouragement.
The knowledge I gained from my time
at Digby Stuart College has
been incalculable,
and for this my gratitude to
Ann Camp, Jen Lindsay, Gaynor Goffe,
and the other tutors.

Contents

Introduction

HE word *calligraphy* is derived from the Greek words *kalli* and *graphia*, and simply means 'beautiful writing'.

Since the earliest recorded times, humans have used art to express themselves. We have examples of primitive paintings and carvings, some which may be as old as 50,000 years. However, the first form of 'writing' dates back 5000 years to Sumeria.

This Sumerian writing style was known as Cuneiform and was formed by making wedge-shaped marks in soft clay. These early 'letters' were symbolic representations of objects, or pictograms. Later, the symbols became more stylised to speed up the writing process.

Egyptian writing, on the other hand, was written on papyrus with either feathers or reeds. Like Cuneiform, the system was based on a series of symbols, but later an alphabet emerged of single letters.

The Chinese, of the same period, wrote on paper (which they had invented), with fine brushes, as they still do. Their flowing brush strokes differed considerably from the rigid Cuneiform.

As language became more sophisticated, the symbolic letters were replaced with letters that represented sounds. Only the Chinese persisted in their usage of pictograms.

The Phoenicians, a Semitic people from Syria, trading around the Mediterranean after 1000 BC, influenced the Greek alphabet with their own. In turn, the Greek alphabet was incorporated into the Roman alphabet, which is still the basis of our modern typefaces or bookprints.

Today's calligraphy students, however, may not realise the debt of gratitude that we owe to the participants in the arts and crafts movement which flourished in Victorian England for translating the secrets and techniques of the scribes of centuries before.

William Morris was foremost in this modern renaissance. He was a designer of wallpapers, fabrics, tapestries and furniture, before he turned his attention to typefaces. He began to study old manuscripts, of which he was an avid collector, and copied the writing styles he found, as well as the richly decorated letters.

His ultimate ambition was to produce his own books, and to this end he established the Kelmscott Press at Hammersmith beside the River Thames in London. The books he produced were elaborately embellished by modern standards, but reflected his love of all things mediaeval.

Although his work served to revive an interest in writing, still little was known of the techniques used by the scribes of hundreds of years before.

Edward Johnston was born in 1872 and because ill health prevented his continuation of medical studies, he decided to devote his attention to calligraphy.

He was helped in his efforts by those who had worked with William Morris, notably Sydney Cockerell and William Lethaby. Johnston was encouraged to study the manuscripts in the British Museum to find inspiration. Through meticulous research, Johnston deduced that the form and weight of the letters were determined by the tools used to write them. Thick and thin strokes were formed by a reed pen or quill, cut to a chisel-edge and held at a consistent angle to the guide lines. He also found that the letter sizes were in direct relationship to the width of the nib, which provides us with the system of measuring the height of letters so they are in correct proportion.

In Victorian times, the accepted practice had been for letters to be outlined with a pointed nib and then filled in. However, Johnston reasoned that this method would have been laborious and too time-consuming for the production of books in mediaeval times when scribes were expected to write several pages each day.

Johnston's studies also led him to explore methods of gilding (applying gold leaf) and the use of decoration to add importance to capital letters at the beginning of sentences.

His classes in calligraphy at the Royal College of Art in London, proved so popular, that it became necessary to print teaching sheets, and then in 1906 his book *Writing and Illuminating and Lettering* was published. It is still regarded as essential reading for those interested in the art of calligraphy, for it shows us in great detail, the end result of his years of painstaking research and experimentation.

HOW TO USE THIS BOOK

Some people are fortunate enough to have a natural uniformity and rhythm in their handwriting which produces beautiful writing. However, most of us are not that lucky.

The purpose of this book is to teach the beginner how to use the edged pen to produce attractive, legible letterforms in the basic styles of Roman, Foundational, Uncial, Italic and Rounded Gothic. The book will provide you with sufficient knowledge of these important alphabets to enable you, with practice, to create your own greeting cards, posters, place cards, jar labels, menus, invitations and much more. You will find so many applications for your new-found ability, and I hope it will whet your appetite to proceed even further with the art, because there is no limit to what calligraphy has to offer. It is a skill which combines discipline with creativity, tradition with innovation and frustration with satisfaction.

I have designed this book so that the alphabets are arranged in a chronological sequence, related to their historical development. You should follow the sequence in order to understand the history behind the letters and to obtain maximum benefit.

Do the practice strokes before attempting the alphabets so that your hand becomes used to the shapes of the actual letters. Follow the stroke sequences shown around the letters. Then, when you feel confident and comfortable with the letters, start writing words. This way you will learn about spacing at the same time.

However, a book, no matter how good, is no substitute for a good teacher. So if you are really keen, try to join a class. Once you master the basic techniques, I can promise you a lifetime of enjoyment and fulfilment in the art of calligraphy.

Part One

PREPARATIONS

Materials

Before you can begin to write, you must first have the correct tools as the quality of your work will be greatly influenced by the equipment you use. It is always a good policy to buy the best you can afford without paying for elaborate equipment which may not be necessary. Seek advice from someone you know who has learnt calligraphy, or from a reputable supplier who understands exactly what you require. Obviously, as you become more proficient there are many more items which you will need to buy. However, to begin with, all you need is a drawing board, ruler, ink, pens, pencils and paper.

DRAWING BOARD

Your first requirement is a suitable drawing board. If you can afford to buy one, there are many to choose from, with or without inbuilt ruling equipment. However, you can improvise by making your drawing board from a piece of laminate shelving board, particle board or something else sturdy enough to support the weight of your arms. Make it large enough to give you plenty of room on which to write — approximately 50 × 40 cm is comfortable.

RULER

You will need a good bevel-edged ruler, sturdy enough not to bow and not less than 40 cm in length. Make sure it has small but accurate divisions which are easy to read — metric measurements are best. I have also found a small ruler, about 20 cm long, very useful for small jobs like addressing envelopes.

T-SQUARE

If you do not have a ruling attachment on your drawing board, you will need a T-square to ensure that all guide lines are precise.

INKS

For practice, use a black non-waterproof ink such as Quink or Higgins. I prefer a liquid Chinese ink and recommend

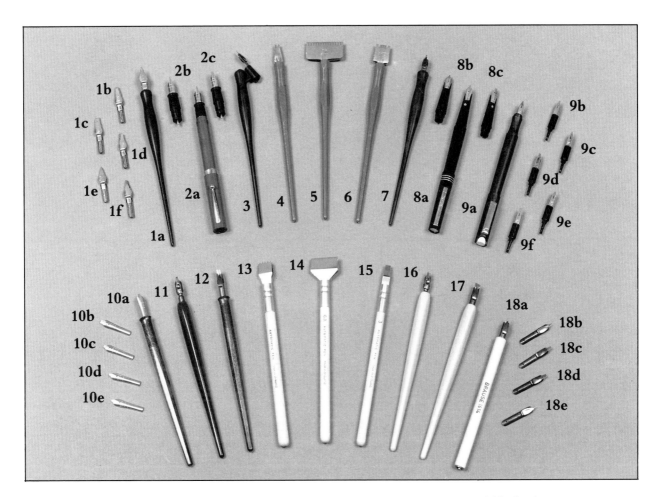

la–f Speedball C-Series holder and nibs

2a–c Sheaffer No-Nonsense calligraphy pen and nibs

3 Speedball elbow holder with copperplate nib

4 Coit pen N-6 ³⁄₁₆″

5 Coit pen 1 ½″

6 Coit pen N-10 ½″

7 Speedball handle with Brause nib

8a–c Osmiroid calligraphy fountain pen with nibs

9a–f Platignum calligraphy set

10a–e Osmiroid dip pen holder with 22 carat gold-plated nibs

11 Speedball pen holder with William Mitchell round hand nib

There are many pens available for the calligrapher. The above photograph shows some of the more popular and unusual types you can buy.

12 Osmiroid pen holder with Brause nib

13 Automatic pen with music nib

14 Automatic pen #6A 1″

15 Automatic pen #3 ³⁄₁₆″

16 William Mitchell triangular plastic pen holder with Brause 5 mm nib

17 William Mitchell triangular plastic pen holder with Brause 5 mm nib

18a–e Brause double-edged wooden pen holder with Brause right oblique nib set

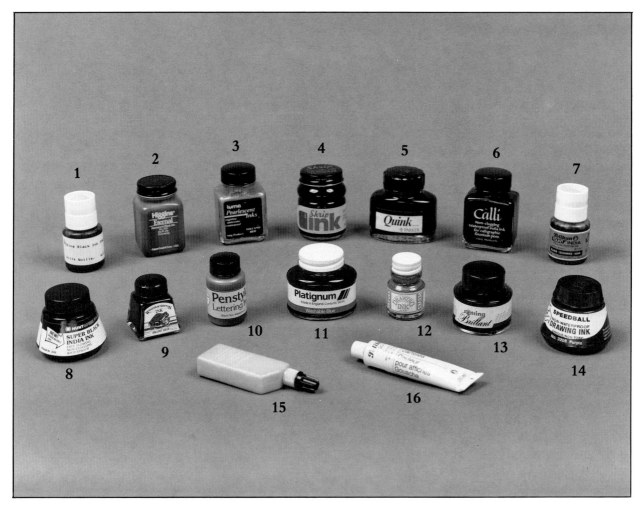

*The above photograph shows a selection of
the vast range of inks available to
calligraphers.*

1	Will's Quills Chinese ink
2	Higgins Eternal
3	Luma Pearlescent (16 colours)
4	Sheaffer Skrip
5	Parker Quink Ink
6	Calli ink (6 colours)
7	Pelikan Fount India ink
8	Hunt Super Black India ink
9	Winsor & Newton drawing ink
10	Rexel Penstyle Lettering ink
11	Platignum calligraphy ink
12	Reeves drawing ink
13	Rotring Brillant calligraphy ink
14	Speedball non-waterproof drawing ink
15	Pelikan drawing ink
16	Pelikan Gouache

it for students because it is a dense black, is non-waterproof (so it washes out of your clothes if the worst happens) and is inexpensive. However, it may not be readily available in country areas.

PENS

There are many types of pens from which to make your choice. Fountain pens, either with a plunger fill or inserted ink cartridge, provide an easy and convenient method of writing. Many calligraphers carry one with them all the time, to use instead of a ball-point — it certainly improves the handwriting. The beauty of these pens is their accessibility and the convenience of not having to depend on having an ink pot nearby, as they carry their own ink supply.

However, if you are really serious in your effort to learn calligraphy, you need to master the dip pen as soon as possible. The relationship between pen, ink and paper is crucial to learning and requires practice to achieve a feeling of harmony.

PENCILS

You should only need HB and 2H pencils. The HB is a medium grade for rough layouts and quick work. The 2H pencil is used for ruling guide lines — being a harder lead, the lines will not smudge so readily.

PAPER

Selecting suitable writing paper is always a problem because there is no way of knowing, without testing it, whether the ink will run, or the texture will make writing with a small pen impossible. The best idea is to contact a specialist shop selling calligraphy equipment and ask the advice of someone who knows the properties of each type of paper.

There is so much variety in make and quality that it is difficult for the beginner to make a choice. Often your local printer will give away off-cuts which you can try, and then you can ask him to identify any which seem suitable. Never decline the offer of free paper — you will use it one day.

Normally, a ream of good quality bond paper from your local stationer will last you for ages. Perhaps you could even share with a friend or fellow student. Some people are lucky enough to obtain free supplies of computer print-out paper which they find suitable for practice.

Setting up

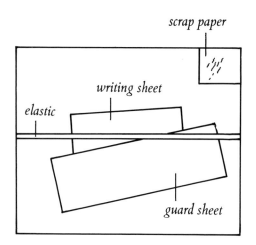

scrap paper

writing sheet

elastic

guard sheet

First adjust the drawing board on your work surface. You can place a brick or block of wood underneath to bring it to the best angle for your needs. You should be able to see the writing clearly and not be hunched over it. It is comfortable to write with the board resting on your lap, leaning against the table — this is often a good idea where space is cramped, such as in a classroom.

Cover your board with a large, flat sheet of blotting paper to add sponginess to the surface. Perhaps you can add a few sheets of newspaper underneath the blotting paper as well if necessary. Do not try to write on a hard surface as you will not achieve a good result.

Next place a strip of elastic, approximately 2 cm wide, around the width of the board. Make sure it is firm but you are still able to move the elastic up and down the board. This will hold your writing page in place, but allow you to move it down as you write. (When you are ruling guide lines, attach the paper firmly to the board with bulldog clips or masking tape, so you can measure guide lines accurately. Before you begin to write, however, release the paper so you can turn it to the most comfortable angle. It will then be held in position by the elastic around the board.)

Place another piece of paper across the width of your page, below your hand, as a guard sheet to protect your work from the grease and moisture on your skin. Another piece of scrap paper can be attached to the top right-hand corner of the board. This is used to test your nib after each dip in the ink bottle to remove excess ink and make sure that the nib is functioning properly.

Getting started

First you need a quiet and pleasant environment as free from interruption as possible. The bench or desk height should allow you to sit comfortably with your feet resting flat on the floor and your forearms supported by the sloped drawing board.

The writing paper can be turned slightly to a suitable angle for ease of writing, so do not fix the paper to the board — the elastic will hold it in place. You do not want to be restricted or cramped, so adjust the paper whenever necessary. Rest your non-writing hand lightly on the paper.

The pen should be held comfortably between the thumb and forefinger, resting on the middle finger. It is best to cure any unorthodox method of holding the pen at the beginning and learn the correct way before you experience difficulties which will discourage you from continuing. Do not grip the pen too tightly. It only needs to be held firmly enough to stop it slipping in your hand. There is no need to exert pressure to form the thick strokes because the pen does it for you. All you need to do is guide it.

Lighting is important and should come from over the left shoulder for the right-hander and the opposite, of course, for the left-hander. It is important to position yourself so you can clearly see what you are writing.

Arrange inks, nibs, pencils and other materials on the side where they will be within easy reach. I am always surprised to see students who actually reach across their work to dip into the ink and risk leaving a trail of ink spots on their writing.

Music can help you to relax and feel the rhythm of the writing. Some music can be helpful, but beware of anything jarring or sharp — it will show in your work. (Mozart is wonderful if he is to your taste, but vocals are distracting.)

The correct way to hold a pen.

Left-handed calligraphy

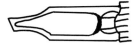

Osmiroid Italic oblique nib

Many left-handers become discouraged after the first lesson. However, with perseverance, they can develop a unique character in their writing which is very attractive and the envy of many right-handers.

Nibs are available specially cut at an oblique angle to make it easier to hold a pen at the required angle. However, you will have to experiment to find the most comfortable position for yourself.

Try turning the page so that the left-hand corner of the page is much higher than the right. You may even need to turn it to an angle of 90 degrees.

Also, some people find that holding the pen with the thumb parallel to the barrel is helpful.

Have you tried writing right-handed? Strange as it may seem, I have found that some students find that they can handle an edged pen more easily with the right hand, even though they may normally write left-handed. It is certainly worth a try.

Writing position for left-handers.

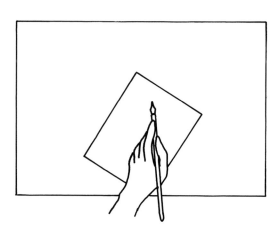

Handy hints

- Insert a piece of foam into the neck of your ink bottle (just far down enough to come into contact with the ink). This will prevent you from dipping your pen in too far, and will cut down on messy blobs on your work.

- When carrying ink, always check that the lid is screwed on securely and then place the bottle in a plastic bag.

- Replace the lid of your ink bottle when you stop work, even just for a short time. It can avoid accidents and prevent the ink from drying out.

- Thin your non-waterproof ink with distilled or boiled water rather than with tap water. Bacteria present in the tap water will grow in the ink.

- If you attend a calligraphy class, try to leave a spare bottle of ink at the teaching venue.

- It is always a good idea to keep a small jar of water nearby and dip your pen in it occasionally to keep it free of ink build-up which will clog the nib. This is particularly important when using waterproof ink. Wipe your pen with a scrap of lint-free cloth or paper. Do not use facial tissues as these tend to shed small fibres. Remember to clean your pen when you stop working, regardless of the type of ink you may be using.

- If you stop for a meal or a snack, remember to wash your hands before resuming work. Grease on paper spells disaster.

- After deciding on a final layout, the time has come to do the piece of work. It is a good idea to do two pieces in case one is spoiled. (Often the guide lines for both can be ruled together if they are placed side by side.)

- Whenever you feel particularly pleased with a piece of work, keep it for posterity in a portfolio. It will be a record of your progress and can also be used for showing prospective clients or employers in the future.

- Keep a scrapbook of ideas which you will find in magazines, newspapers, books and so on.

Nomenclature

Learning any subject is made easier by understanding its nomenclature, or terminology. Without a basic knowledge of nomenclature you will find it difficult to comprehend the more advanced calligraphy textbooks where alphabets are analysed. These few simple examples should prove helpful.

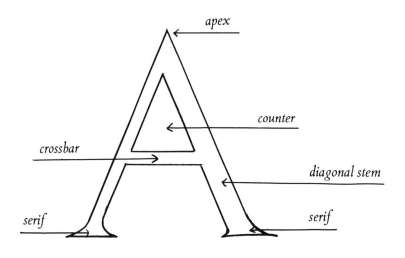

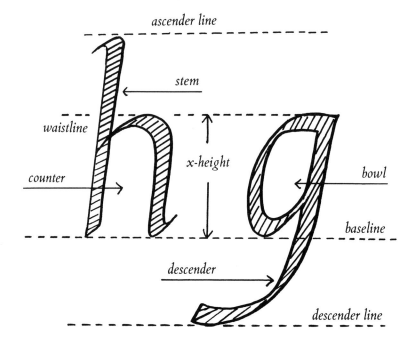

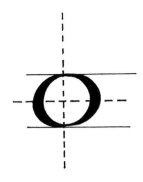

Horizontal bias.
Pen held at 30 degrees angle.

Diagonal bias.
Pen held at 30 degrees angle.

tt ra æ tr

Ligatures (joining letters).

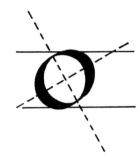

abcdefghíj
klmnopqrs
tuvwxyz-ab

Interlinear spacing is the space between the lines of letters.

Serifs.

club　　*bracketed*　　*hooked*　　*slab*

Ruling guide lines

I have not provided printed guide lines in this book because I believe that it is best to learn to prepare them yourself. This way, you are able to have the writing any way you wish, and it helps you to understand the reasons for the spacing of the lines.

The distance between the guide lines is variable, according to the style of the letters, whether it is majuscule or minuscule (capital or lower case) and, most importantly, the size of nib you are using.

The permanent guide sheets I am about to describe will be held underneath the writing sheet so the guide lines show through for you to follow, for the practice strokes. If you use a heavy smooth paper or light white board, your guide sheets will be more durable. Rule the lines with a black ball-point or technical pen so that you will be able to see them through the page.

However, when you come to write your special piece, you will need to rule up temporary guide lines, in pencil, directly onto your writing sheet. When you have finished writing, and the ink is dry, then you can rub out the pencil lines.

The size of the lines will depend firstly on the letterform you are using, whether it be Roman or Uncial and so on. Each style has its own particular line spacing which it requires to enable the lines of letters and words to be seen clearly. Secondly, the size of the lines depends on the size of nib you use. A small nib produces small letters while a large nib produces large letters.

When you prepare each guide sheet it is a good idea to write the pen size, letter style it is for and the measurements on the sheet so you will be able to identify them in future.

When learning a new style of writing it is necessary to learn by using a large nib so you can clearly see how the letters are formed. A small nib does not have such clear differentiation between thin and thick lines.

PEN WIDTHS

The correct and proportional height of any letter is measured in pen widths. To do this, turn your nib so the writing edge is vertical, and then make a series of straight strokes, one above the other in a diagonal line, just touching each other with no overlapping, and build up to the required number for each style.

For example, for Roman capitals, the height of the line required is seven pen widths, and you will also need adequate space between the writing lines to allow you to see the letters clearly, so leave about another four pen widths in between the actual writing lines.

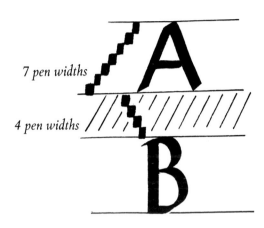

Foundational, because it has ascenders and descenders, needs more space to allow for the extra height and length of the strokes. You will need to prepare the guide sheet with a line height of four and a half pen widths with seven pen widths between the writing lines, so that the ascenders and descenders do not intertwine.

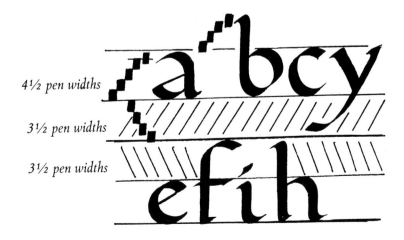

Uncial, being a majuscule or capital alphabet, can be written in quite closely spaced lines. To begin with a line height of five pen widths with another five in between the lines, will permit comfortable spacing.

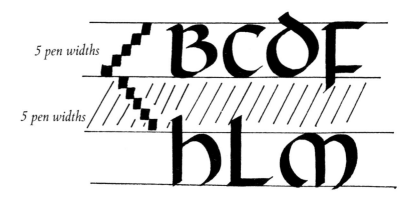

Italic can be set out in a similar fashion to Foundational with a line height of five pen widths and a space between the lines of ten pen widths to allow room for the ascenders and descenders.

Since Rounded Gothic is written five and a half pen widths high, with ascenders of three and a half pen widths in height, the double writing lines need to be eight pen widths apart.

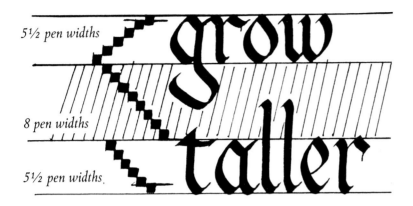

You must always use these pen widths to gain the correct proportion while you are learning. The size of the letters will depend solely on the size of the nib you are using. Later, when you have more experience of the basic alphabets, it will be possible to vary these proportions to obtain other effects, but it is necessary to learn this correct method first.

Getting to know your pen

To become friends with your pen you will need to spend time discovering what your pen can do for you. These decorative borders are formed by holding the pen at a consistent angle to the line, and building up the design. You will enjoy doing these exercises and they will be useful to retain in your portfolio. You never know when you might be able to use them as decoration.

Part Two

LETTERFORMS

Roman

The Roman alphabet is the most widely used and easily recognised of all lettering styles because most of our modern typefaces are based on it. The capital letters have been used for over 2000 years and are still models of good design which have defied attempts to distort them. It remains the ultimate alphabet.

The alphabet represents the development of several centuries, from the early Sumerian pictograms through the Phoenician alphabet adopted by the Greeks, whose letters were in turn used by the Romans as a basis for their writing.

The supreme example of the classical Roman alphabet is found in the incised letters of the Trajan Column in Rome, dated circa AD 114.

Roman letters, as seen on Trajan's Column in Rome, circa AD 114.

SENATV
IMPCAES
TRAIANC

The variations of light and heavy strokes occur when a square-cut pen or brush is held at a consistent angle to the guide line. These inscriptions are believed to have been first painted onto stone with a chisel-edged brush to provide a guide for the stone cutter.

The characteristic shapes of the Roman letters were echoes of the architecture of the same period. Imagine the rounded arches of an aqueduct, the graceful columns of the public buildings, and you will find these in the curves and precisely angled letters of this alphabet which endures as lasting evidence of the grandeur of ancient Rome.

For their visual impact, Roman capitals depend on careful proportions, based on a square and half square. In the first exemplar, the skeleton form of the alphabet is shown to demonstrate the proportions as they relate to a square. Use a pencil to draw these until they become familiar.

Note the positions of the crossbars in their relation to the centre line. Pay careful attention to proportions.

PROPORTIONS OF ROMAN CAPITALS

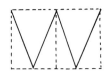

The letters O and Q are a full circle (the width of a square), while C, G, and D fit within 7/8 of a square.

These letters fit within ¾ of a square.

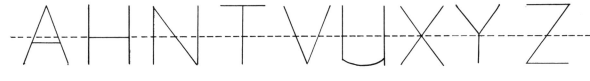

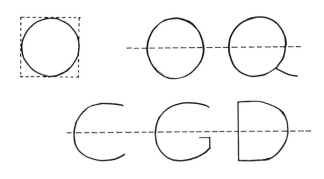

M is slightly wider than a square.

W is the width of two letter Vs.

½ square letters.

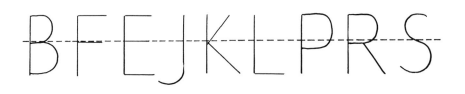

Practise several rows of these strokes, keeping the nib at a 30° angle. If you are holding the pen correctly, the same angle will be seen at the base of the stroke also. Try to keep the stokes straight and even.

Hold the pen at the same angle and draw diagonal strokes. Keep them straight and aim for consistency. Note that this stroke is thicker than the verticals on the first line.

At the same 30° angle again, draw diagonal lines in the opposite direction. This stroke is the narrowest which you have drawn.

These horizontals will be the crossbars of your letters and should be narrower than those in the second example, but wider than those in the third. Note the pen angle at the beginning and end of each stroke.

Practise these curved strokes, again holding the nib at a 30° angle. Do not attempt to force the nib. Once the stroke reaches its narrowest mark, stop. The next stroke will come to meet it.

Reverse the curves you have just drawn, with the pen at the same angle. Now you have formed the two strokes of the letter O.

Let us put them together and try O. Note that the first stroke begins below the top line. Os require lots of practice.

Start

Many people try to space Roman capitals mechanically, carefully measuring the width of the letters, and inserting uniform space between letters. Then they wonder why it does not look correct. This is because, while some letters have obvious boundaries, which the eye accepts, for example H and N, many others have open spaces like C, L and T, which need to be considered when arranging letters visually to produce even spacing.

As a general rule, curved letters are placed closer together, while letters with vertical downstrokes like I, H and N are placed further apart to allow the eye to see sufficient white space between them.

MIND HOW

VISUAL

MECHANICAL

HIND

Wider spaces between vertical strokes.

SOON

Less space between curved strokes.

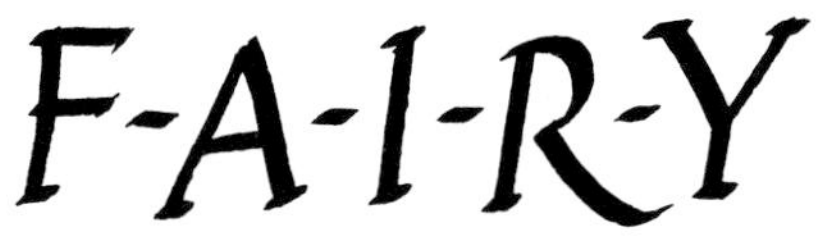

F-A-I-R-Y

Wider spacing suggests lightness.

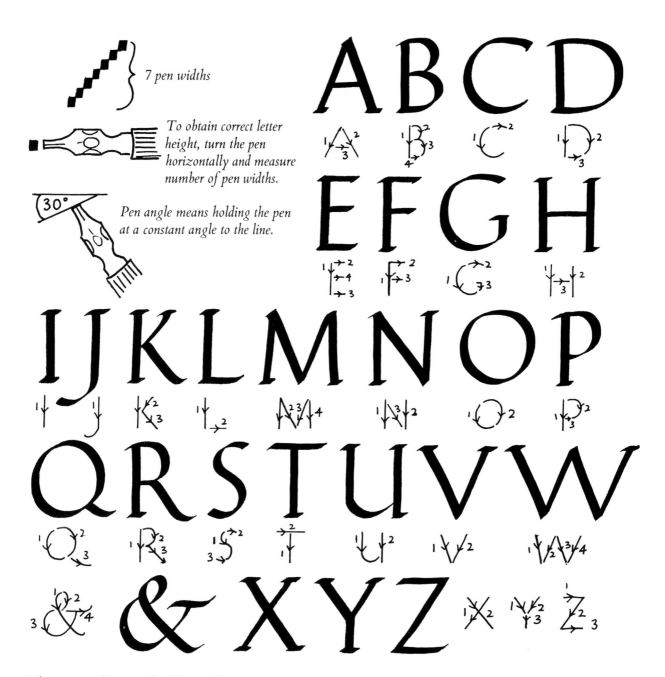

7 pen widths

To obtain correct letter height, turn the pen horizontally and measure number of pen widths.

Pen angle means holding the pen at a constant angle to the line.

ABCD

EFGH

IJKLMNOP

QRSTUVW

&XYZ

These numerals are used with capital or majuscule letters — all the same height.

1234567890

GREATNESS
IS TO TAKE THE COMMON THINGS OF LIFE AND WALK AMONG THEM

OLIVE SCHREINER

Foundational

The Foundational alphabet originated from the ninth century bookhand (style used for books) called Carolingian Minuscule. It was developed by the English scribe, Alcuin of York (*c.* AD 735–804), under the direction of Charlemagne. For the present, however, we have to thank Edward Johnston for enabling us to understand how these letters were written.

The art of writing with an edged pen had been lost for many centuries and Johnston realised that the letters were not drawn and filled in but written freehand. Otherwise, how could a complete Bible be produced by such a tedious method in mediaeval times? The answer was that the shape of the pen dictated the shape of the letter.

English Carolingian style in the Harley Psalter.

mundaprıuſ
quodıntuſ

Through studying old manuscripts to find a writing style which would be easily recognised by those used to a lower case Roman style, he decided that the tenth century minuscule letters used by Winchester scribes of that period would be most suitable. The Harley Psalter (Manuscript 2904 in the British Museum) provided the best example of this and it became the basis for what Johnston would later call his Foundational hand.

This style is included in the book because of its importance in the understanding of calligraphy, and in learning it, you will become aware of the joy of writing with an edged pen. Because the letters are based on a circular O, this alphabet is rounded and weighty owing to its being only four and a half pen widths high.

It is a generous alphabet, so remember that its full shapes will take up more space than you realise. Do not try to cramp it.

The Roman alphabet is suitable to use as capitals with the Foundational minuscule or lower case letters.

PRACTICE STROKES

Hold the pen firmly with the nib at an angle of 30° to the writing line. All curves are part of a circle, so keep them rounded, four and a half pen widths high.

Practise these generous curves starting just below the top line, then proceed to right-hand curves.

Practise these right-hand curves, but remember to stop when the nib resists. Do not force it.

Join both curves to form the letter O. Practise plenty of these — they are very relaxing!

These important straight strokes begin and end with a continuous round movement.

The top curve becomes a straight stroke. Then it is lifted off with the same circular movement as in the previous exercise.

4½ pen widths

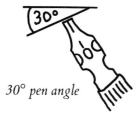

30° pen angle

strong arch

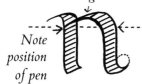

Note position of pen

Be aware of change from curve to straight line — slow down for this.

abcde

fghijkl

mnopqrstuvw

xyz &

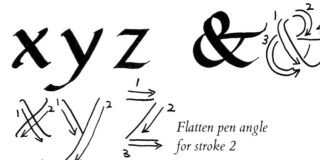

Flatten pen angle for stroke 2

These numerals are used where the text is predominantly minuscule or lower case, such as Foundational. Note that the number one sits on the baseline. Follow the same stroke sequence as for the Roman majuscule numerals.

1234567890

'Terror!' 'Dead heat!' they were shouting –
　　　'Terror!' but The Screamer hung out
Nose to nose with Holy Terror as across
　　　the creek they swung,
An' M' Durmer shouted loudly, 'Put yer
　　　tongue out, put yer tongue out!'
An' The Screamer put his tongue out,
　　　and he won by half–a–tongue.

EXTRACT FROM
'GROG-AN'-GRUMBLE STEEPLECHASE',
BY HENRY LAWSON.

Uncial

The Uncial alphabet became the main Roman bookhand by the fourth century AD and is associated with the early Christian church. Its name is probably derived from the Latin word *uncia* meaning 'inch', and can be written comfortably in that size.

Early Uncial written with pen at 0 degrees angle to the line.

PLICITER ETTCAROMEA

Insular half-Uncials.

aduehiat reghum

The Uncial letterforms are more rounded than the Roman capitals — E, T and M take on circular shapes and some letters have small strokes, which extend beyond the writing line. Many students find this confusing, because we are used to separate upper and lower case typefaces, and do not accept a majuscule alphabet which appears to have ascenders and descenders.

To increase the writing speed, gradually a minuscule alphabet developed called Half Uncial, and this became divided into different regional styles as the monks spread the Christian gospel throughout Europe. Most notable examples are the Insular styles of England and Ireland which produced the famous *Lindisfarne Gospels* and *The Book of Kells*.

Uncial letters were usually written with the pen held at a very flat angle, or in some cases, parallel with the writing line (at 0 degrees). The result was a rounded letter with heavy down-strokes and light cross-strokes.

In the following exemplar I have used a later form of Uncial which the student should find easier to handle. It is not historically accurate for any specific period, but conveys the *feeling* and appearance of the later style.

You will find it useful for many purposes, but do remember its history, treat it with respect, and do not use it to advertise garage sales and parties!

PRACTICE STROKES

111111111111

Holding the pen at 30 degrees, begin with a small hook and draw a series of straight lines. Try to keep them evenly spaced.

CCCCCCCCCC

Now, draw curved strokes, remembering that this alphabet is round and generous, so don't skimp on the shapes.

))))))))))

The opposite curves will join to form full circles when combined with those above.

1111111111

Now, practise diagonals. Hold the pen firmly and enjoy the rhythm.

ナナナナナナナナナナナ

Combine diagonals with horizontal strokes.

OOOOOOOOO

Try to form circles. Note the thin and thick areas of the letters. You may need to check the pen angle.

EEEEEEEEE

This Uncial letter is different from a Roman 'E'. Remember to keep it round — it is part of a circle.

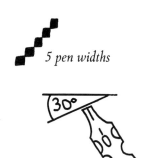

5 pen widths

30° pen angle

These letters are round and generous, so think 'circular'.

ABCDE

FGhIJK

LMNOPQRST

UVWXYZ&

alternates AE

1234567890 ;?!

Flatten pen angle for stroke 2.

HE MAKETH ME TO LIE DOWN
IN GREEN PASTURES;
HE LEADETH ME BESIDE
THE STILL WATERS.
HE RESTORETH MY SOUL:
HE LEADETH ME IN THE PATHS
OF RIGHTEOUSNESS
FOR HIS NAME'S SAKE
YEA, THOUGH I WALK THROUGH
THE VALLEY OF THE
SHADOW OF DEATH, I WILL
FEAR NO EVIL:
FOR THOU ART WITH ME.
THY ROD AND THY STAFF,
THEY COMFORT ME.
THOU PREPAREST A TABLE
BEFORE ME IN THE PRESENCE
OF MINE ENEMIES
THOU ANOINTEST MY HEAD
WITH OIL: MY CUP
RUNNETH OVER.
SURELY GOODNESS AND
MERCY SHALL FOLLOW ME
ALL THE DAYS OF MY LIFE,
AND I SHALL DWELL
IN THE HOUSE OF THE LORD
FOREVER......

PSALM 23

Italic

This style of lettering was developed in Italy during the Renaissance, and, like Foundational, was an adaptation of the Carolingian Minuscule used in the ninth century in northern Europe. It was rounded in form and became the basis for the later Roman minuscule.

With the advent of printing in the fifteenth century, this style became the model for typefaces. However, there was still a demand for handwritten manuscripts, where only one or a limited number were required, so a more cursive, or quickly written style was developed, called Chancery Cursive, now commonly called Italic.

The letters became compressed and the rounded O became elliptical. Often the writing had a slight slope and sometimes the ascenders and descenders were elaborately flourished. Writing masters began producing manuals containing detailed instructions for mastering the intricacies of fine writing.

The most notable of these writing masters was Ludovico D'Arrighi who published his *Operina* in 1522. This form of writing became popular throughout Europe and was used by Queen Elizabeth I of England.

Lettering after the style of Ludovico D'Arrighi.

stretto da molti amici
riguardo hauendo al=
do non solamente' di
eri anchora, volessi
scriuere, et regulata=
teri e note' delle' lre'
di chiamano noletier

The following exemplar is an informal Italic alphabet which does not require a great number of pen lifts and many of the letters can be joined for faster writing. There is a more formal Italic which is written more slowly and with higher branching in letters such as M, resulting in rounded arches.

The purpose of the following practice is to help you to develop rhythm and freedom. Italics are light and lively so relax and enjoy these exercises. Hold the pen lightly at an angle of 45 degrees.

PRACTICE STROKES

Slide the pen up and down without any pen lifts. Note the thick and thin strokes.

Use a slight slope — no more than 10° from the vertical — and begin and end each stroke with a small hook of the pen.

Alternate long and short strokes, trying to maintain uniform slope and spacing.

These strokes should spring from the base of the previous stroke. Keep the pen on the page.

Now try the clockwise version of the above. You will need plenty of practice in these arching strokes.

5 pen widths

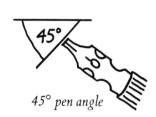

45° pen angle

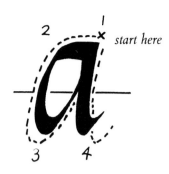

start here

Practise these anti-clockwise strokes first.

acdefgijloqtuy

acdefgijloqtuy

bhkmnprsjvwxz

pivot here

bhkmnprsjvwxz

Italic minuscule numerals

1234567890

A B C D E

A B C D E

F G H I J K

F G H I J K

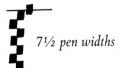

7½ pen widths

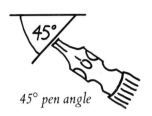

45°

45° pen angle

These letters are slightly taller, sloped and narrower than Roman capitals.

L M N O P Q R S T

L M N O P Q R S T

U V W X Y Z E &

U V W X Y Z E &

Italic majuscule numerals

1 2 3 4 5 6 7 8 9 0 ;?!

How sweet the moonlight
sleeps upon this bank!
Here will we sit,
and let the sounds of music
creep in our ears
Soft stillness and the night
become the
touches of sweet harmony

WILLIAM SHAKESPEARE

ABCDE

A B C D E

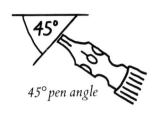

7½ pen widths

45°

45° pen angle

FGHIJK

F G H I J K

Never use Swash (decorative Italic) capitals for entire words as they are too hard to read.

LMNOPQQRS

L M N O P Q Q R S

TUVWXYYZ

T U V W X Y Z

When daffodils
begin to peer
With heigh !
the doxy
over the dale
Why, then comes in the
SWEET
O' THE YEAR

Rounded Gothic

During the twelfth century in Europe, we find that min-uscule writing started to become more compressed, so that on the page its appearance was heavy, dark and with the density of a textured pattern when seen in a mass. Hence the style was called *Textura*, from Latin meaning 'woven'.

In addition, as more and more people sought education it became necessary to produce books more quickly and economically. So a style of writing which was relatively easy to write, and could be squeezed into less space became more desirable. However, while this Textura writing served the purpose, its main drawback was its illegibility.

Variations of this style appeared throughout Europe, but in countries in the south, particularly Spain and Italy, the scribes managed to combine the heavily vertical Textura with roundness, and developed a style known as Rotunda, which was in use until the late Renaissance period, particularly in northern Italy.

In northern and central Europe the Textura style remained popular for many centuries, and when Gutenberg invented movable type in 1450, the first typeface was in this style. Today, it is still found in the official documents of some countries.

The Rounded Gothic on the following sheet is a composite Gothic style which echoes the characteristic angularity of Textura, but is softened by curves. The result is attractive and rhythmic letterforms which are more useful to the calligrapher where legibility is a prime requirement. This alphabet will be a valuable addition to the calligrapher's repertoire for use in instances where an *olde worlde* style is called for.

*Pen angle should be approximately 50°
and the curve has a slightly angular look.*

*The opposite curve has the same
characteristic shape, and will join the other
to form an O.*

*Join the two retaining the sharply pointed
top and the diamond-shaped counter in the
middle. This will appear in other round
letters. Try to keep the top and bottom of
the letter in line so that it does not appear
to be toppling over.*

*Straight strokes begin and end with a slight
curve.*

Rounded Gothic numerals.

1 2 3 4 5 6 7 8 9 0

5½ pen widths 50° pen angle

a b c d e f g h
i j k l m n o p q r s t u v
w x y z   *alternate forms*   ꝗ v w x ſ

8 pen widths 50° pen angle

A B C D E F G
H I J K L M N O P Q R
S T U V W X Y Z &

In Remembrance — Lest we Forget — In Remembrance

Part Three

DESIGN FEATURES

Choosing the right style

Your choice of lettering style can set the mood for the message you wish to convey. You would not consider using a heavy style such as Rounded Gothic to suggest something light and fairy-like. Nor would the impressive Uncial look appropriate for a bargain sale sign. A knowledge of the history of these styles will help you to decide the most suitable. Here are a few ideas which may be useful.

Roman requires concentration. It is disciplined, visually satisfying and well constructed — like Roman buildings. The Roman alphabet is most suited for headings and emphasis. It suggests elegance and classic style, and requires generous spacing to be seen at its best.

AUSTERE
CLASSICAL
DIGNITY
QUALITY

Foundational needs to be written more slowly. It requires plenty of space, so do not cramp it. Its generous proportions ensure its legibility and it is surprisingly versatile. You will also find many instances where it can be written with a slight slope once you become more proficient. This will give it a more modern appearance and extend the possibilities for its use. Because it is so easy to read it is very good for place cards, names on certificates, labels, and anything which needs to be read quickly.

Legibility
solidity
weighty
generous

Uncial needs to be treated with proper respect. Now you know its history you will understand why. Because it also looks old-fashioned, it is most useful for commemorative projects and work of a religious nature. It is a capital alphabet so it can be written in closely spaced lines with great effect.

CELTIC
MEDIEVAL
EASTER
ANCIENT

Italic is probably the most versatile of all the lettering styles, and can be adapted for almost any purpose. There are so many variations which can be explored once you have learnt the basics. Informal Italic can suggest dancing, movement and freedom, whereas the less cursive, upright style

freedom

movement

d-a-n-c-i-n-g

formal

is used for formal wording. You could even surprise your friends with a beautifully written letter in Italic.

Rounded Gothic is an important looking alphabet which is also best used to suggest antiquity. It is not to be overdone or it becomes less interesting and hard to read. It is good for titles and dominant words, but it needs to be combined with another style to provide a contrast. It can be used for an *olde worlde* look or to convey a sense of importance to certificates.

importance
olde worlde
Christmas
Certificate

Layout tips

The layout is the most important element in the design and presentation of your work. Good lettering can be ruined by poor layout but a pleasing layout can make mediocre lettering look almost professional, particularly when seen from a distance. For layout do's and dont's, see page 74.

When planning your layout it is essential that you allow sufficient space all the way around the page. On a single page layout (the most commonly used) the side margins are equal, but for a double page spread, the two pages are treated as a single unit, so the inside margin is halved. Here are a few layout ideas.

Double page — see how the centre margin is equal to the side margins. The margin at the bottom of the page should be approximately twice that left at the top of the page.

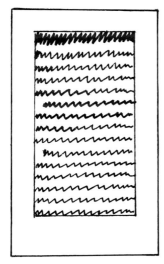
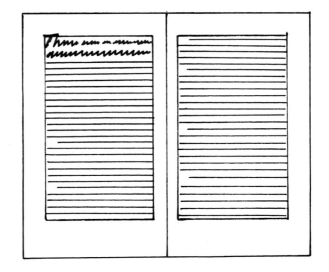

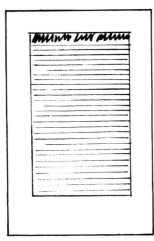
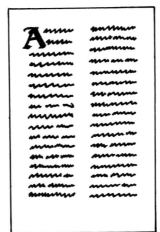
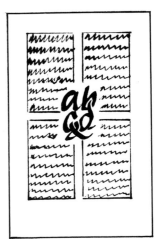

Decorative layout

It is valuable to practise arranging your work in a decorative way. It will develop consistency and rhythm if you are careful to keep the slope and spacing even. Use different sized pens for contrasting weight and texture, but remember to always measure the correct, proportional height in pen widths for each nib you use, be it large or small. Make friends with your pens. See what they can do for you and enjoy the relaxation of just playing with the possibilities.

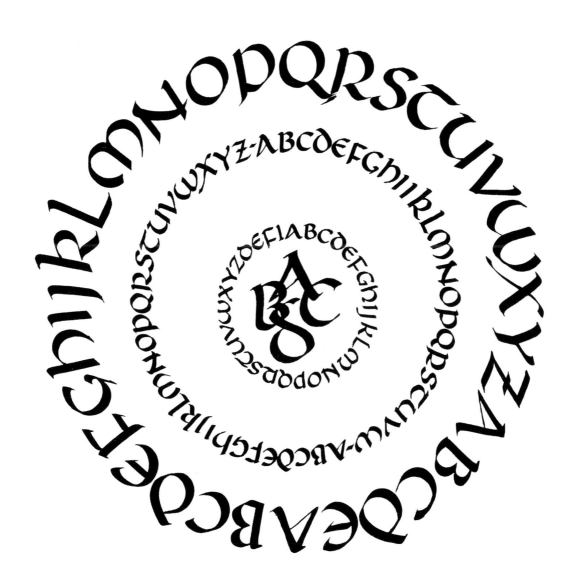

March dust on apple leaf brings all kinds of fruit to leaf.

If apples bloom in March, In vain for'un you.... May you eat'un míche and pap.... apple bloom in March, if apples bloom in March, in vain for'un you'll sarch, If apples bloom in April, when they'll be plentiful, then they'll be plentiful.

An apple a day keeps the doctor away.

September, blow soft, till all the apples are in the loft.

If apples apples bloom in March, in vain for'un you'll be plentiful

—waves·waves·waves·waves·waves·

come fly with me, come fly with me, come fly with me

come fly with me, come fly with me, come

come fly with me, come fly with me·—

Have fun with your pen

Some common errors

At the beginning of lines you need to consider the shape of the letters, particularly in the case of capitals, and line up the text visually so that the letters appear to be in line, rather than in mechanical fashion.

Spaces between words should only be sufficient to ensure separation to make them readable. The space of the counter in an O is sufficient. Any greater distance than this can cause a problem as rivers of white space form vertically in lines of text, as shown here:

No
Bother
Here

Vertical strokes lined up.

Correct spacing will prevent these rivers of white space in your text.

Some
Letters
Cause
Problems

Visually adjusted alignment. See how curved strokes extend beyond the guide line.

See how
→Odd this
Looks
Now

The curved letters appear out of line.

Texture

One element of calligraphy not often considered is the texture formed by the relationship of letter strokes to spaces in the text.

Where legibility is not the prime concern, a dense, weighty texture can convey strength and power and add interest to the design. However, more widely spaced lines of writing will improve the legibility and create a lighter texture. Experiment for yourself and see how many different effects can be achieved.

Variations in texture can be obtained in several ways, such as:

Making the pen angle flatter to produce heavier strokes, or reducing the writing height.

Compressing the letters.

austere and
restrained in
his manner,
accustomed

CHARISMATIC
CHARISMATIC
CHARISMATIC
CHARISMATIC
CHARISMATIC
CHARISMATIC

Altering the interlinear spacing. This will allow more or less white space between the lines of writing.

Varying the intensity of the ink by diluting it to give a transparent effect. This can be used as a background for other letters.

Backgrounds

Backgrounds add an extra dimension to your work. You can create an attractive and interesting background for your work by simply using a carpenter's pencil or a double pencil. When you write with them, no gaps appear between the letters. You may like to try using two coloured pencils or ball-point pens for added interest.

DOUBLE
PENCIL

ELASTIC BAND

CARPENTER'S
PENCIL

Special pens and effects

Once you feel comfortable with ordinary dip pens, you will want to widen your horizons and there are many varieties of interesting pens and lettering tools available. The range of automatic pens allows you to write much larger letters, or with a double line, or there is even a five-line music pen. There is a large range of sizes and you will enjoy exploring the possibilities they offer. For suppliers see the list at the back of this book.

If you need to write large letters and you do not own a suitable writing tool (with a large enough nib), it is possible to obtain an exciting, spontaneous look by using a double pencil (two pencils held together with an elastic band) or even two coloured ball-point pens or felt-tip pens. For even larger letters, a matchbox slipped between the pens will allow you to write letters with an x-height of 23 cm. If you wish, these can then be filled in with colour, using a brush.

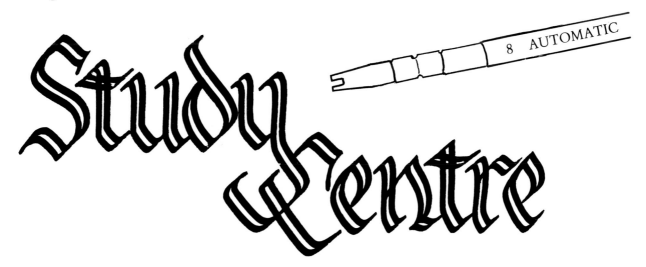

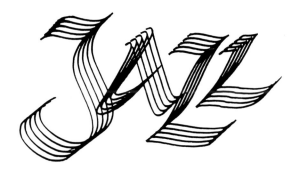

Fill in with brush.

Automatic music pen

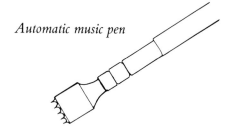

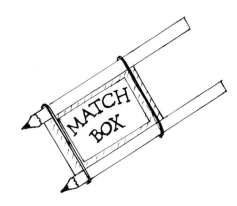

Use elastic bands to attach pencils either side of a matchbox.

Decorative motifs, borders and flourishes

Use a fine pen to draw your own decorative corners, borders, motifs and flourishes. Try to develop a few on a single theme and then file them in your portfolio. You will use them one day.

Decorated letters

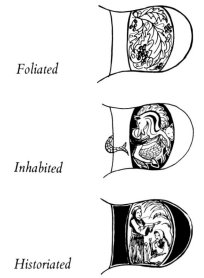

Foliated

Inhabited

Historiated

Decorated letters can be great fun to create. Write a few basic capitals, say in Roman or Uncial, with a large pen. Then using a fine nib, begin 'doodling' around the shapes of the letters. Keep them simple to begin with, then add curleques and lines, accentuating the shapes of the letters. As you feel more confident you can begin to outline some capitals with your pencil and practise drawing shapes until you are comfortable with them. Fill in the broader areas with shapes of flowers, leaves or abstract designs.

Elaborate decorated capital letters have long been a feature of the handwritten manuscript and you will enjoy designing appropriate ones. They can be mediaeval in character, art nouveau or modern — the choice is yours.

Shown here are examples of historiated, foliated and inhabited letters.

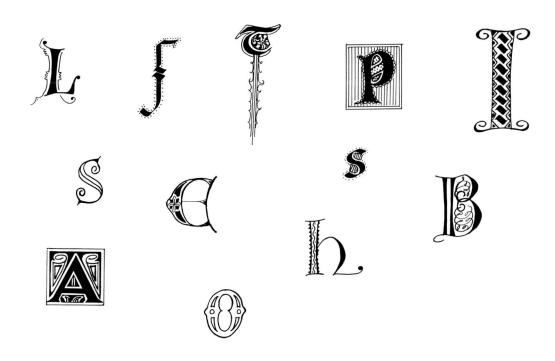

Using colour

Nothing will enliven your work more than the discriminate use of colour, but some understanding is needed before proceeding. Early manuscripts featured capital letters written in vermilion (bright red) and this provided an exciting contrast to a mass of black text. It is very tempting, however, when faced with the astonishing array of colours available, to use too many in one piece of work. Remember that tints and shades of a colour can be obtained by the addition of white or black.

Coloured paints generally available, come in the following groups.

Using a small watercolour brush, feed the colour into the space between nib and reservoir.

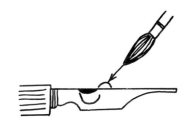

Speedball nib — feed from above.

INKS

These can be further divided into waterproof and non-waterproof. Waterproof inks contain shellac, and you will need to clean your pen frequently to prevent it clogging. There are some good brands of calligraphy ink which give a dense vibrant colour, but usually in a limited range of colours. Drawing inks can be used but they do not possess the opacity of calligraphy ink.

WATERCOLOURS

These come in pans or tubes and a liquid concentrate suitable for writing. Their transparency can produce beautiful effects, but they can only be used on white or very light backgrounds.

Mitchell nib — feed from underneath.

POSTER COLOURS

Always readily available and in a good colour range, poster colours may be bought in jars or tubes. They cover well, are inexpensive and can be useful for quick lettering work, but are not suitable for quality pieces.

DESIGNER'S GOUACHE

This is a good quality, finely ground paint which is very suitable for calligraphy because of its opacity and covering qualities. It is necessary to mix it to a writing consistency and you will need to develop the technique of feeding the pen with a small brush but the effort is well worth while as it gives the calligrapher an unlimited range of writing colours and expands the choice of backgrounds, so that coloured papers and boards can be used.

STICK INK

Chinese stick ink is available in several good colours, and requires grinding with an ink stone before use.

FELT PENS

These can be obtained in many different widths and colours and are ideal for quick posters, price tickets, and so on. They can be used to great effect, but fade quickly, particularly in shop windows. To work out a rough design they can be the designer's best friend.

Part Four

CALLIGRAPHY FOR EVERY OCCASION

Posters

Once you become more adept at calligraphy, one of the first things you may be called on to do is to prepare a poster for your favourite charity or fund raising group. Writing skills are always in demand to publicise events and it is a good exercise to attempt it. You will be encouraged when you see your own handiwork on public display.

When presented with a mass of wording for the poster, you will need to decide what is important and what can safely be eliminated. The main message should dominate the page and be sure to include such information as time, place, directions and admission charge (if appropriate).

THUMBNAIL SKETCHES

A series of thumbnail sketches will help you select the layout which works best. Try different weights of writing by using a heavy pencil or felt-tip pen to simulate the lettering. Remember that the optical centre is slightly above halfway, so the bottom margin is greater than the top.

It is important to have the most important words written in a sufficiently heavy weight to allow them to dominate the other writing. Select a pen at least two sizes larger to give that contrast.

Use a pencil to draw roughs of several thumbnail sketches of your layout, trying different ways to arrange the blocks of wording of differing lengths to create interest.

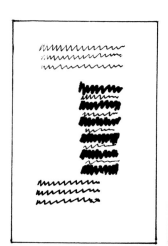 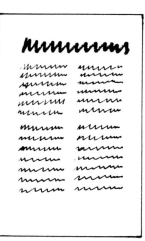 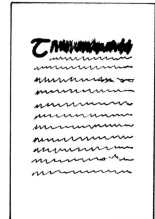 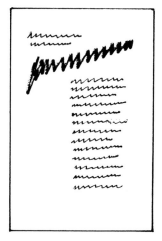

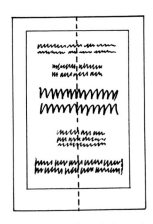   

Symmetrical — balanced on centre line.

Asymmetrical — aligned on left margin.

Asymmetrical — balanced areas of text and space.

Incorporate space for any artwork at the planning and paste-up stage.

PAGE LAYOUT

To visualise the finished work it is best to prepare a paste-up or rough copy. First, write out the most important words with a large pen, paying attention to spacing. Next, write out the remaining blocks of text using smaller pens. It will probably be necessary to try a few different sizes in order to achieve the contrast needed.

Break up the lines of text into suitable phrases and cut them out as close as possible to the letters and place them in position on a sheet of layout paper measured to the required dimensions and marked out roughly with the layout plan. Use spray adhesive for this step, as it will allow you to re-position the wording strips.

When you are satisfied with the layout, measure the line spacing and transfer these measurements to the final sheet. Then you can begin on the final poster.

For a symmetrical or equally balanced layout, rule a centre line vertically down the middle of the page and fold the cut-out wording strips in half, placing the fold on the centre line. This will allow you to centre the text exactly on the page.

Any artwork or cut-out illustrations should also be included here as an integral part of the layout, not added later as an afterthought just slotted into a space. Asymmetrical layout requires careful planning to achieve unity and balance between the text areas and the spaces. Probably, it is best to begin by using the symmetrical layout.

LAYOUT DO'S AND DONT'S

- *Do* list your subject matter in order of importance.

- *Do* delete any unnecessary wording which will only confuse the reader.

- *Do* keep the readers in mind. What will appeal to them? Are you aiming your display at adults or children? Where will the poster be seen?

- *Do* make sure that the main message dominates the work. It may be the event itself, the sponsor, time or place.

- *Do* divide the text into small blocks, smaller than the main message.

- *Do* make a few small rough (thumbnail) sketches of the layout to see which one works best.

- *Don't* let it become too fussy — where ornament is concerned, less is better. You will get the message across more effectively if you keep it simple.

- *Don't* use too many colours. It will take you longer to write and will not improve the poster.

- *Don't* skimp on margins — they are an important part of the layout.

SPRINGWOOD ART CENTRE
will hold a

Craft
Market

Saturday and Sunday next
13th, 14th August...10 to 4 p.m.

DEVONSHIRE TEAS SERVED DAILY, HOME-MADE CAKES,
POT PLANTS & HERBS, CONFECTIONERY, JAMS, PRESERVES,
KNITWEAR, CROCHET, WEAVING, CERAMICS, CANEWARE.

Come and support the work of our local craftspeople.
See demonstrations, films and buy quality products

POTTERY
Watercolours
OIL PAINTING
Quilting
PATCHWORK
Calligraphy
HERBS
Potted Plants

L·O·N·S·D·A·L·E · C·R·A·F·T

C·E·N·T·R·E

Letters and envelopes

Probably the most appreciated application of writing is found in a letter to a loved one. Here you can practise your Italic using a small edged pen (for this a fountain pen is most useful) and give pleasure at the same time. Pay particular attention to layout, making it as interesting as possible, perhaps incorporating some colour and shape for added appeal. You could consider using a theme for your layout (see the examples) which will capture the reader's attention immediately. Carry the theme through to the envelope and give not only the lucky recipient a thrill, but the mail sorter and the postman as well!

Coloured notepaper and envelopes are readily available, but some papers, particularly those with a diagonal texture, do not provide a suitable writing surface so it is best to buy one or two first and try them out. Remember to use appropriate colours whether they are cool colours like blues and greens from one end of the spectrum, or the warm pinks and hot reds and oranges from the other.

Watch for attractive stamps as they are issued. Some on current issue may not suit the theme of your letter or may not complement the colour scheme, so keep a supply of different types on hand.

Springwood,

Just a note to let you know that I expect to arrive about two o'clock tomorrow afternoon - leaving here at eight a.m. and will be calling in to visit the family at Moss Vale for a

My Dear Friend,

quick lunch. I'll bring those books which I promised you some time ago and we shall be able to revive lots of memories of the time we spent at the old school. The enrolments for the new course are coming in gradually, and we hope to start the week after next. Your niece contacted me to submit her name already, so she will have a busy semester with all her other commitments. She seems to fit such a lot into each week - I am always surprised to hear how much she has achieved both in her career and on the family front as well. Weather here has been glorious, particularly for mid-winter. The climate in this part of the mountains is really ideal - no heavy frosts as occur in the upper mts. I am so looking forward to seeing you and spending a few days with you in your new home. See you soon

Affectionately,

Ann

MY KINDRED SPIRIT

How much you would have enjoyed with me
my visits to see all the new Tasmanian Potteries
Never have I seen such delicacy, refinement, and
flawless exquisite mirror glazes with almost sublime
simplicity of design. What a tactile medium of art
is pottery! I longed to caress each beautiful and shapely
piece I encountered. It is indeed some time since I have seen
such meticulous workmanship and vitality in rich abundance

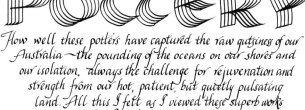

How well these potters have captured the raw outlines of our
Australia — the pounding of the oceans on our shores and
our isolation. Always the challenge for rejuvenation and
strength from our hot, patient, but quietly pulsating
land. All this I felt as I viewed these superb works
of craft. How I wish you and all my loved ones
had been there to see and share these delights
perhaps we can all be together again soon

FONDEST WISHES

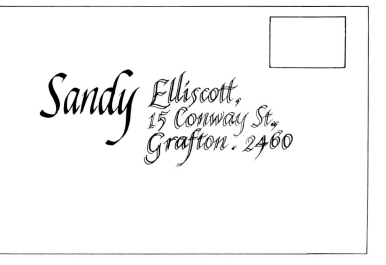

Sandy Elliscott,
15 Conway St.,
Grafton. 2460

JIM BELANGER
51 HIGH ST.,
GEELONG 3220.

PLEASE DELIVER TO.....
Pamela
306 View St.,
Glenbrook 2773.

Greeting cards

Single fold

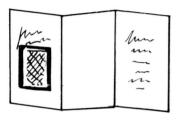

Double fold

French fold

Many people are deterred from making their own greeting cards because they believe that they have no artistic ability. However, you can produce unusual and exciting cards for any occasion with just a little imagination and the minimum of equipment. Your own calligraphy can provide a multitude of decorative effects, and a few are included on the following pages to assist you.

Blank cards are usually available from printers. Check that the envelopes are the correct size to accommodate the cards. Postal regulations may dictate the maximum size envelope for the usual postal rate, so beware of those over-sized cards unless you are prepared to pay extra to send them.

You may prefer to use paper to make your cards, and there are many methods of folding the paper. The simplest ways are illustrated here.

For a single fold you will need board or heavy paper that is stiff enough to stand up. However, if you prefer a double, or even a French fold, the paper can be much thinner as it requires two folds. The card can be reproduced by photocopying, if you use this method and design the layout correctly.

Wrapping paper and printed artwork are a great source of decoration ideas. Always be on the lookout for interesting designs with a small repeat pattern which you can cut out and mount on the front of the card. Add your own calligraphic message and there you are — an original, one-of-a-kind greeting card.

Peace on Earth

A gift for You

Be Happy

Thank you

happy birthday

Congratulations

WE'RE MOVING HOUSE

HAPPY NEW YEAR

GET WELL SOON

Especially for you

HAPPY BIRTHDAY

Christmas wishes

Certificates and place cards

At some stage, you may be asked to write names on certificates or place cards, and the following technique will enable you to position them correctly.

First, you need to decide on the correct pen size to use. On tracing paper write a few names with different pens, perhaps using two different lettering styles, and place each one over the certificate. When you have selected the one which looks best, write all the names on a piece of paper, lining them up at the left-hand edge, making sure that the spacing within the words is correct. Then mark out measurements across the page as shown in the diagram.

If you jot down the length, it is a simple matter to divide that in half and mark the centre point of the line. This will sit on the centre line of the certificate, and the length can be lightly marked on either end. Practice will improve your judgment to allow you to make small spacing corrections as you go along, but if you have warmed up first by writing out the names, you will find that the final lengths of the words are almost identical to your practice run.

It is also a good idea to ask for a typewritten list of names and check the correct spelling before you begin, to save any mistakes.

Use the same method for place cards.

Mark Williams 9
David Randall 9
Joy Blakeney 8
Joan Marshall 9
Kay Nixon 7
Susan Veness 8
Gregory Johnson 11

3 4 *Centre* 5 6 7 8 9 10 11 12

Centre

Marking out measurements to correctly centre text.

centre line

Retail tickets

Attractive price tickets reflect the quality of goods displayed and calligraphy can be used to great effect in merchandising.

Labels

Even a jar of home-made jam takes on a special quality when decorated with a hand-lettered label. You can even use your calligraphy for recipe books, name tags and school project labels.

You can write all your own labels

Nutmegs

Peppercorns

Cinnamon

Curry Powder

Mixed Herbs

Whole Cloves

Green Tomato Pickles

Seville Orange Marmalade

Mango Chutney

Raspberry Jam

Blackberry & Apple

Strawberry Conserve

Bookplates

Bookplates make a lovely gift for special friends. Use a name or initials and perhaps incorporate a simple illustration. Decorative copyright-free borders and patterns are available in books. (See Suggested reading.)

Monograms and ciphers

Here are some examples of using calligraphic initials to form monograms and ciphers (monograms share a common stroke). You may like to design one using your own initials. If you are interested in needlework, the design can be embroidered after tracing the outline onto fabric.

Logos and letterheads

Many business people prefer a logo design for their letterheads and cards, and calligraphy opens up many possibilities. Try different types of pens and styles to find the most suitable.

THE TRAVELLING FAIR

Autumn Festival

Country Crafts

The Tall Ships

roundelay
FOR FINE FOOD
restaurant

Springtime

Gift and other ideas

Kay and Tony

would be pleased to have you share with us
in the Blessing of our Marriage to be held
at St. Mark's Church, Coney Heath on
Saturday, 9th August, 1986 at 4.30 p.m.
This will be followed by a reception
at Coney Heath Village Hall High St.

R.S.V.P...9th July, 1986
34 Tyttenhanger Green
St. Albans. Herts. AL1
Phone . (0727) 32357

Here are some suggestions for using your new-found art.

- Framed poems, quotations, proverbs, religious messages, recipes.

- Recipe book of your own special recipes.

- Personalised bookplates or even stationery.

- Decorated baby's name and birth details for those with a new baby.

- Inserts for wedding albums with details of the event as a wedding present.

- Designs for embroidered initials.

- Designs for personalised T-shirts.

- House name signs.

- Calligraphed documents, such as marriage or birth certificates, title deeds.

- Wedding and party invitations.

- Engagement and birth announcements.

- Brochures and programmes.

- Titles for book jackets.

2 CUPS SELF-RAISING FLOUR, 1 CUP SUGAR,
& 1 TEASP. MIXED SPICE, 2 CUPS MIXED FRUIT

MIX
DRY INGREDIENTS IN
MIXING BOWL ~ PLACE TWO
TBLSPNS BUTTER OR MARGARINE
IN CUP & FILL WITH BOILING WATER.
WHEN DISSOLVED POUR INTO THE DRY
INGREDIENTS. MIX 1 TEASP.OON OF CARB
SODA WITH A LITTLE HOT WATER IN CUP
AND FILL WITH COLD WATER. ADD TO THE
MIXTURE AND STAND OVERNIGHT. IN THE
MORNING BEAT ONE EGG & ADD TO MIXTURE
STIRRING WELL, GREASE STEAMER WELL
1 PUT A CIRCLE OF GREASEPROOF PAPER
GREASED IN BOTTOM OF STEAMER.
SEE SIDES ARE WELL-GREASED, PLACE
IN BOILING WATER BOIL 4 HRS,
ADD BOILING WATER WHEN NEEDED. LEAVE
STAND FOR AWHILE BEFORE TIPPING
OUT ONTO COOLER...

Grandma's Christmas Pudding

List of suppliers

NEW SOUTH WALES

Artdraft
120 Rowe Street
Eastwood 2122
(02) 858 3300

Artistcare
346 Kent Street
Sydney 2000
(02) 29 4151

Artistcare
3 Victoria Road
Parramatta 2150
(02) 683 5300

Oxford Art Supplies
221 Oxford Street
Darlinghurst 2010
(02) 360 4066

Will's Quills
166 Victoria Avenue
Chatswood 2067
(02) 419 6031

VICTORIA

The Calligraphy Centre
962 Whitehorse Road
Box Hill 3128
(03) 898 1101

Deans Art
368 Lonsdale Street
Melbourne 3000
(03) 602 2184

Tafts — The Pen People
Centreway
259 Collins Street
Melbourne 3000
(03) 654 7993

Victorian Artists' Supplies
715 Main Road
Eltham 3095
(03) 439 8798

SOUTH AUSTRALIA

The Calligraphy Centre
61 Hindmarsh Square
Adelaide 5000
(08) 223 3424

Eckersleys
21 Frome Street
Adelaide 5000
(08) 223 4155

Premier Art
43 Gilles Street
Adelaide 5000
(08) 212 5922

QUEENSLAND

The Pen Shoppe
14/16 City Plaza
Adelaide Street
Brisbane 4000
(07) 221 3160

WESTERN AUSTRALIA

Creative Hot Shop
108 Beaufort Street
Perth 6000
(09) 227 8768

Jacksons Drawing Supplies
103 Rokeby Road
Subiaco
(09) 381 2488

Jacksons Drawing Supplies
148 William Street
Perth 6000
(09) 321 8707

TASMANIA

Artery
31 Davey Street
Hobart 7000
(002) 23 2130

Salamanca Place Gallery
65 Salamanca Place
Hobart 7000
(002) 23 3320

J. Walch & Sons
130 Macquarie Street
Hobart 7000
(002) 23 3444

AUSTRALIAN CAPITAL TERRITORY

Arttec Warehouse
30 Lonsdale Street
Braddon
(062) 57 1711

Swains
Garema Place
Civic Centre
Canberra City 2160
(062) 47 8515

Suggested reading

Angel, M. *Painting for Calligraphers*, Pelham Books, London, 1984.

Angel, M. *The Art of Calligraphy*, Robert Hale, London, 1978.

Backhouse, J. (Susan Davis, ed.) *International Calligraphy Today*, Thames & Hudson, London, 1982.

Backhouse, J. *The Illuminated Manuscript*, Phaidon Press, London, 1979.

Briem, S. E. *Sixty Alphabets*, Thames & Hudson, London, 1986.

Camp, A. *Pen Lettering*, A. & C. Black, London, 1984.

Child, H. *The Calligrapher's Handbook*, A. & C. Black, London, 1985.

Diringer, D. *The Book Before Printing*, Dover, New York, 1982.

Dubay, I. & Getty, B. *Italic Letters–Calligraphy and Handwriting*, Prentice Hall Press, New York, 1986.

Fairbanks, A. *A Handwriting Manual*, Faber & Faber, London, 1978.

Gillon, E. V. *Decorative Frames and Borders*, Dover, New York, 1973.

Gourdie, T. *Handwriting for Today*, Pitman/Pentalic, London, 1971.

Gourdie, T. *Mastering Calligraphy*, Pitman, London, 1984.

Gray, B. *Lettering Tips for Artists, Graphic Designers and Calligraphers*, Van Nostrand Reinhold, New York, 1980.

Harvey, M. *Creative Lettering, Drawing & Design*, Bodley Head, London, 1985.

Jackson, D. *The Story of Writing*, Studio Vista/Parker Pen Co., London, 1981.

Jarman, C. *Making Calligraphy Work for You*, Osmiroid, 1985.

Johnston, E. *Writing and Illuminating and Lettering*, Pitman, London, 1948.

Knight, S. *Historical Scripts*, A. & C. Black, London, 1984.

Lancaster, J. *Lettering Techniques*, B. T. Batsford, London, 1980.

Mahoney, D. *The Craft of Calligraphy*, Pelham Books, London, 1981.

Martin, J. *The Complete Guide to Calligraphy*, Phaidon, London, 1984.

Nesbitt, A. *The History and Technique of Lettering*, Dover, New York, 1957.

Neugebauer, F. *The Mystic Art of Written Forms*, Neugebauer Press, Austria, 1979.

Pearce, C. *An Anatomy of Letters*. Taplinger Publishing, New York, 1987.

Pearce, C. *The Little Manual of Calligraphy*, William Collins, London, 1982.

Sassoon, R. *The Practical Guide to Lettering and Applied Calligraphy*, Thames & Hudson, London, 1985.

Shepherd, M. *Calligraphy Projects for Pleasure and Profit*, Thorsons Publishers Ltd, Northamptonshire, 1985.

Svaren, J. *Written Letters*, Pitman, London, 1975.

Taylor, P. *The Australian Calligraphy Manual*, Allen & Unwin, Sydney, 1987.

Whalley, J. I. *The Pen's Excellence,* Calligraphy of Western Europe and America, Midas Books, Kent, 1980.

Whalley, J. I. *The Student's Guide to Western Calligraphy*, An Illustrated Survey, Shambhala Publications Inc. Colorado and London, 1984.

Wong, F. *The Complete Calligrapher*, Watson-Guptill Publications, New York, 1980.

Glossary

Alphabet   Series of letters used to form words.

Ampersand   The abbreviation for *and* based on the Latin *et*.

Arches   The strokes which spring from the stem of a letter, e.g. m or n.

Ascender   A stroke which projects above the writing line, e.g. b.

Base line   (or writing line) The bottom line where minuscule letters sit.

Black letter   A term used to describe a Gothic text which was close-spaced and dark in texture.

Body height   The height of the *body* of a lower case or minuscule letter, not including the ascender or descender.

Bookhand   Any style of writing used to produce books in the days before printing.

Capital   Upper case, majuscule or large, formal letters.

Carolingian   A minuscule script developed by the scribe Alcuin of York, while at the court of Charlemagne.

Chancery cursive   Italic style, used by scribes of the Papal chancery.

Chisel-edged   Describes straight-edged pens or brushes used for writing.

Colophon   An inscription at the end of a book, giving details of the scribe, date, etc.

Counter   The space formed within a curved stroke, such as in a b, c or d.

Cross-stroke   Horizontal stroke as in E, F, or H.

Cursive   Where the letters are joined, as in handwriting.

Cutting mat   A plastic mat specially designed to allow the use of a cutting knife or scalpel without damage to its surface.

Descenders   Strokes which drop below the base line, such as the tails of j, g or y.

Exemplar   An example or model from which to copy.

Flourish   An extension of a pen stroke used to decorate or embellish.

Fraktur   A form of Gothic or Blackletter script.

Gesso   A mixture including plaster which is applied to provide a raised letter for gilding.

Gilding   Application of gold leaf to an adhesive base such as gesso.

Gothic   The heavy Mediaeval script popular in northern Europe which is upright and closely spaced.

Gouache   Fine quality paint which is opaque and can be used for writing as an alternative to ink.

Hairline   A fine stroke executed with the edge of the pen, to form a decorative serif.

Half Uncial   An early bookhand with ascenders and descenders.

Illumination   A term used to describe the decoration of a manuscript.

Ink stone   A stone shaped with a well for grinding stick ink.

Italic   Common term used to describe the sloped script which originated in Italy. It is often called Cursive.

Justification   Spacing of lines and words to achieve uniform length.

Ligature   Joining of letters, often to save space.

Lombardic   A form of Gothic capital letter.

Lower case   Minuscule or small letters, as opposed to capitals.

Majuscule   Large or capital letters.

Minuscule   Lower case or small letters, with ascenders and descenders.

Palette   A white tray used for mixing paint.

Palimpsest   A manuscript which has been erased and rewritten.

Pen width   The width of the writing edge of the pen. A measurement used to determine the correct letter height, found by building up horizontal strokes of the selected pen.

Reed pen   Hollow reed cut in the shape of a pen, similar to a quill.

Rotunda   The rounded form of Gothic script.

Rustica   An informal Roman capital alphabet.

Scribe   A person who writes documents or manuscripts.

Scriptorium   A room set aside, usually in a monastery, for the writing of manuscripts.

Serif   A small stroke used to finish off the end of a larger stroke.

Slope   The amount of angle with which letters are written.

Spacing   The distance between letters, words and lines.

Stem   The main down-stroke of a letter.

Stick ink   Compressed ink in stick form which needs to be ground and mixed with water before use.

Swash   A decorative form of Italic.

Textura   Derived from the Latin, meaning 'texture', it describes a heavy, closely written form of Gothic script.

Uncial   A majuscule Roman alphabet used as a bookhand during the fourth to eighth centuries.

Vellum   A smooth textured writing material prepared from animal skin, usually calf or sheepskin.

x-height   A term used to describe the body height of a minuscule letter, i.e. the height of the letter x with no ascender or descender.

Index